THE PHILOSOPH

BRITISH CAR RESTORATION

ROBERT MOREY

Palmetto Publishing Group, LLC
Charleston, SC

Copyright © 2017 by Robert Morey.

For information regarding special discounts for bulk purchases, please contact Palmetto Publishing Group at Info@PalmettoPublishingGroup.com.

ISBN-13: 978-1-64111-000-6
ISBN-10: 1-64111-000-7

Here goes . . .

As always there are too many individuals and events which have led up to this, to ever possibly list, so I apologize in advance! I dedicate this book to the thousands of like-minded enthusiasts I've encountered over my 43 years in this business . . . this hobby so engrossing and their intensity so infectious. Without Millie "Bentley" Horton, Tom Horton, Erik Calonius, and my wife Michele, the book itself could not and would not have happened. The support of family is so critical as well. Thank you Mom and Todd and son Bob (slipping in the oil of my footsteps).

TABLE OF CONTENTS

INTRODUCTION

WELL, HELLO AND WELCOME TO THE BOOK. I hope you have time to stay
with it awhile, as it's possible you will gain something here! To start, I
should touch on a little bit of my own experience, the "why" of my writing this book—the provenance, if you will, of the aging (but generally
well-lubricated) machine that is me! I live in Charleston, South Carolina,
and have for many years, but as some people have observed I'm "not from
around here." I grew up (allegedly) in Washington, D.C., and it was there
at the formative age of 14, resting after school, that I heard the sound
of a mechanical symphony. This was not the harsh noise of parts doing
battle with each other under the hood of one of my friends' cars; this
sound was purity of a mechanical nature, a symphony, and indeed one
of the greatest icons in the automobile industry from any nation, by any
educated enthusiast's measure—a series one Jaguar XKE roadster, a red
roadster, and from the window of my room, I looked straight at her, at
hubcap level from 30 feet away. A scene like that and that profile, at that
age, left a more dramatic impression than my buddy showing me his dad's
Playboy magazines! I had found something that connected to every point
on my compass of desire. It not only looked absolutely incredible, but it
was making sounds, beautiful harmonious sounds that didn't whisper a
hint of speed but proclaimed it loudly, like a one-two punch!

A few weeks later a neighbor down the street brought home a 1962
Powder blue Triumph TR4 and parked it facing our house. I felt as though
it stared at me through those big headlights each day as I arrived home
from school and it also seemed to be calling to me! Could something that
cool ever be mine? I began imagining myself arriving at school in her
and the looks of envy I would no doubt receive from the other kids in

their parents' Ford Granada or some other now long-forgotten vessel of boredom . . . . And like waking from a pleasant dream, I still own and drive that car today! She has covered around 600,000 miles as of this writing, not a bad reward for a young teenager for frantically mowing yards for a few weeks to gain the then princely sum of $125 to secure the deal! I knew I was having fun but had no idea how all this was going to become the focal point of my coming career!

Charleston cobblestones and a vintage car, not great for the suspension....

I met the driver of the E type, Shilo, who saw my rapturous enthusiasm. I'm sure actually he couldn't miss it: it would be like not seeing the fire engine in your living room! After making sure this rabid kid had all his shots and didn't bite, he took me under his wing. In a short time I had my driving permit and drove the TR4 (having paid that princely sum of $125 in cash!) all of 200 feet home myself! Shortly thereafter, I was hired as an apprentice at Mountjoy's Auto Shop in Hyattsville, MD, where Shilo was a mechanic. There I was thrust into a world of Aston Martins, Austin Healeys, Triumphs, MGs, Jensens and the marque that became the focus of my personal collection, Lotus cars! All was well for a few days as I became oriented to the job. Shilo and I would car pool and he would try to educate me a bit about the British car trade before arriving at that Mecca of mechanical marvels! About a week went well . . . . I was not ready for the first, and to this date the worst, "oops" in the history of my automotive career.

The back of the building, with doors where the cars are moved in and out, slopes steeply down to a fairly busy street. One of the real mechanics tossed me the keys to a red Spitfire that was just inside the door. I started the car and engaged reverse. Easing out the door, the car rolled swiftly down towards the road. I saw traffic coming and pressed what was supposed to be the brake, and the pedal slapped down to the floor like it wasn't there at all! The prospect of being rammed broadside by the rapidly approaching vehicles, now a second or two away, led me to a snap decision to engage first and re-enter the garage, which saved me from the broadside but hurtled me into a service area crowded with customers' cars in various stages of disassembly. Rather than hit two, I steered for a Mini up on jack stands; the resulting crash sent the Mini to the floor and folded up the bonnet of the poor brakeless Spitfire! I was fired on the spot. My career had, it seemed to me, been crushed like the cars in front of me, but as the details of the event unfolded, I was retained!

When I left Mountjoy's for the Jaguar dealer in my new hometown of Charleston, S.C., I even left with a letter of recommendation in hand! There, I met a man I still refer to as my mentor, Sam Van Norte. He seemed to know everything and no book was necessary; he just seemed to know intuitively what made it go and what made it give up. I wanted to be like him! He was the service manager there at Charleston Lincoln Mercury Jaguar Rover Triumph MG Fiat, and at the dealer there was even a guy teaching employees mechanical theory—classroom style.

I was astonished how much more "relaxed" things were at the Jaguar dealer than I could have imagined (in retrospect I know what I was seeing was the difference in lifestyle from Washington, D.C. and Charleston, S.C.). My salary was more than my high school counselors had ever even hinted at; my shop mates were friendly and helpful; and many good memories were made! Tricks of the trade were handed down liberally and all seemed rosy . . . except . . . the car industry being what it is is . . . well, unreliable . . . and the dealership closed. Luckily, I was under Sam's wise wing, and he negotiated to take a few mechanics over to the Datsun dealer (yes Datsun—that does show my age!)

Now my previous training as a high-end mechanic was useless; here, little meaning was attached to our toils. There was and is no elegance attached to the Japanese, "grocery getter" car business. I'm not suggesting the fellows who designed them were not wise; quite the contrary! They have made their cars the world's envy for reliability, but this isn't about that! . . . . The practical jokes and general hooligan-like behavior in the shop gave me a feeling like I had to be somewhere else. Some of it was fun, but, in telling a few of those memories of my brief departure from British cars (at least during my day job), I will carefully leave out the names (I still live here and that dealer is still open!). It's no secret that people are generally skeptical of dealers and "fearful" would be a word appropriate at the pay window . . . . It's what goes on you don't know about, that you don't want to know about . . . well . . . maybe you do!

I walked into the shop one day which is a long garage wide enough to pull cars into bays on either side of the garage, and in the center of the garage, hung a large banner with the images of some happy Datsun owners with their new cars, or some such malarkey. But I had walked in from the mechanics' side of the building and could not see the " happy" people on the banner; I saw the back of the banner where there was a "blue" movie being shown from a projector on a mechanic's tool box! Another day I heard "Lookout!" yelled down the shop, followed by the impact of a hockey puck into the side of a customer's car with a loud "clang" and the resultant dent in "slightly too thin" Japanese metal.

Still another day I was greeted with the sight of a new Maxima lying on its side in the undercoating bay where the lift had malfunctioned. Once I was asked to hand a mechanic a wrench from his workbench, as I passed. What I didn't know was that he had run a wire from the coil of the car he was working on (I use the term "working" very loosely) to the steel workbench, and as I touched the wrench, he spun the starter of the car. With the coil rigged to the steel workbench and my hand on the wrench, I experienced a mind-altering version of an electric chair. I vibrated for a few days after the convulsions subsided and still view ignition coils with a bit of apprehension and get nervous when there's lightning.

Last occasion I have to relate to you from there—though there are many others and quite a few might result in legal proceedings or at least some angry phone calls!—is the occasion when I observed one of my shop mates drill a hole into the toolbox of a mechanic who was not in that day and install a grease nipple into the side of the toolbox. Now some of you know that many large garages have huge drums of grease which travels through special pipes in the building to the service bays. The system is usually powered by compressed air and delivers amazing volumes of grease in short order . . . as was the case with the interior of the aforementioned toolbox. What a mess he found on returning to work: the grease was oozing from all the seams on the box. At least nothing would rust . . . .

I had to get away from all that, and the fact was, I made more money working at home on weekends than at the Datsun dealer all week.

The British sports car owners I had met at the Jag dealer were always dropping by, and I acquired a reputation for being the "go to" guy for those that really loved their cars. So, I opened the first of my shops specializing in British sports cars! Sam was my window into the future of what my life would become as a mechanic, and he made a fairly strong effort to steer me away from this less-than-desirable form of employment. Right as he certainly was, I stayed and, although I might have been lucky in some less cancerous, less thankless, more profitable career, you know like collecting matchsticks or train spotting . . . , I have nonetheless made the most of it and at this age there is no turning back. As a matter of fact, I am now something of an "elder" in the game and, having survived these many years and so very many "trials by oil" in the industry, I am now in the enviable position to display my laurels (Yes, right here!) and then promptly lie down on them . . . . Thank you Shilo. Thank you Sam. Here in this book is what I've learned (or imagined . . . ; keep in mind, I did get hit in the head a few times and breathe a lot of chemicals and exhaust fumes . . . !)

So, now you know a little about early Robert Morey, but why should you listen to his thoughts on the psychology and philosophy of British cars? Well, let me tell you a little more! Of course like everyone, my views are skewed in the rearview mirror of life! As I strain to think back the many long years of sports cars and try to recall all the throttles that have passed under my foot, I have been involved either in part or in complete control of the restoration, maintenance, and repair of Aston Martins, Austin Healeys, Bentleys, Rolls-Royce, Ferrari, Lamborghini, MGs, Triumphs, Land Rovers, Lotus, etc.

I have restored and competed in concours nationally with Jags, Lotus, Triumphs, an Allard, and one Ferrari of my own. Since that tender age of 14, British cars have been a passion, fostered by my father and mother who helped me buy my first and still my current ride, that Triumph I spoke of.

I have worked in some fine shops, including Mountjoy's Auto Shop, where I saw my first British racing cars and first laid eyes on the cars that would make my heart flutter still to this day. Mountjoy's made me an apprentice and from there I worked at Charleston Jaguar Rover Triumph MG Fiat. I also spent a year at Webb motors in Virginia, a virtual time warp MG dealer, now a restoration shop and sales center for those gems of history for which my heart beats fast. From there I owned British Auto Service in Charleston, S.C., which became so large at one point that my business partner or I would come in early in the morning to discover new Jaguars left on the lot for warranty work, the owners thinking we were the dealer, which was actually a few miles up the road. I then started and for many years owned Exotic Auto in Myrtle Beach, S.C., and it was from that platform that I was able to make the money I needed to finally own my dream cars instead of just repairing and restoring them for others. I finally got to dive into restoration of the great icons for myself and, of course, other people, and it paid well too! From that shop I have photos of four XKE series one roadsters in simultaneous restoration! And it was there in Myrtle Beach that I met the famous Joe Grimaldi, long time sports car racer and entrepreneur who showed me the power secrets from the British sports cars' heyday, with much emphasis on Jag and Lotus.

My Long time friend Bob Lane (with his Allard I built)
being interviewed for television at Amelia island.

Nowadays, I operate at a much smaller pace and in a smaller shop and have decided to pass along to you, my good reader, some of what I learned, for there is nothing so powerful as knowledge (although a well-built series one XKE feels like a winner!) The big feather in my cap was having a restoration I did of an Allard for the Bob Lane collection in Charleston invited to display at the Amelia Island Concours d'Elegance in 2011.

So I hope I am of some service to you and you soon feel the road moving under your wheels with the melody of a finely tuned machine.

Cheers,
Robert Morey

SECTION 1:

PHILOSOPHY
AND PSYCHOLOGY

And how does this make you feel?

We are told by psychologists not to think of our cars as extensions of our personality . . . . "Bull"! That is exactly what we like and want to do; the car you drive is the most visible and convincing way we, the people, state who we are, what we like, think, desire. We that have deeper pockets and matching long arms can even use cars as some use clothes, matching our moods with the car: a sober coupe with limited abilities when a somber mood swings low like the proverbial chariot and a dashing red roadster when hormones are in abundance and the whole world seems fresh and exciting! A car can tell your story to an audience without you uttering a sound--the history of your family, the pedigree of your family tree.

Overlooking the Battery, Charleston S.C.

I have even seen cars adorned with a heraldic coat of arms. Are you a scoundrel dressed in black, low and stealthy or a movie star, all flash and bright red? Our cars do something for us more than take us on our chores. Many a collector reflecting his loves and prejudices, his or her genetic origins or family history, might rarely or perhaps never display his treasured automobile, so for the shrinks to suggest that we are committing some error, they have in fact made a mistake themselves. There is more to this hobby than any one book or person could ever understand and indeed it is different for each person and changes its meaning with the changes in one's path of life . . . but I will try to make sense of at least the basis of this book, the British Cars! Lie back now on the couch and let me point out some commonalities I have observed in my many years at this, not always gospel but "commonalities" certainly . . . . British car owners tend to own several cars at once and usually, but not always, the same style. An MG owner is likely to have several MGs, for instance, but not likely a Triumph . . . . An enthusiast for Rolls-Royce could easily have a Bentley in the garage or vice versa! Lotus owners are very likely to have had many Lotus in the past or have them all at once! All the cars instill a passion and, like collecting paintings by Matisse, the owners cherish them and put forth a great deal of thought in acquiring and housing them. Most collectors seem to favor a time period and that is almost always the 60's and, to a lesser extent, the 50's, and these, by most accounts, can be described as the "golden years" of the British car! Other commonalities are the tendency to imbibe, have a boat or airplane; the high likelihood is that the individual concerned is something of a adventurer, a person willing, and indeed likely, to forgo the safety of the path taken by life's lemmings but more inclined to that road less traveled (my goodness we are a cool lot!) Also it is far from unusual to find as much money or more spent to house a car as to purchase it, or them—black and white checkered floors and large pieces of art of many forms and definition such as antique gas pumps and full wall murals depicting famous race tracks, a bar made to appear like or in fact being an ancient part of a pub, still stained by a thousand past pints. (I myself suffer from an old "beer injury" where my right hand clenches as though holding a bottle! Often I will tell my friends when pondering some mechanical difficulty, "I don't know, I guess I'll have to sit down and 'drink about it.' ")

And what all this love of British cars does for us transcends words. I have often sat silent in the company of a knowing collector friend and just admired the sweeping lines of some metallic beauty he or I have saved from "times crusher," and in so doing comes another part of this story—why we do this. Some people do this to preserve history and truly feel that this is a selfless service to generations to come. Those inclined to save an old Jag from certain smelting think themselves doing a greater service than saving something less svelte. The cars we love, we do feel to be art or at least a snapshot, if you will, of a time loved, and in the saving of a collector car, a time not "lost"! In that train of thought, I would like to point out that some collectors lean heavily toward cars of a specific year, 1964 by example. It might be the year of your birth or the year you were married and it has meaning deep. Perhaps the year of significance is 1967, "The Summer of Love." Many would argue this to have been the pinnacle year of all British collector cars and with good reason: the following years US federal requirements severely damaged everything from horsepower to headlamp aesthetics, but that is not the thrust of this book . . . . We do this to feel good about something, ourselves, our parents, a past lover, a scene from television? Emma Peel from the series *The Avengers* driving her Élan or Maxwell Smart in his Sunbeam or inspector Morse in his Jag? The car can connect us to something—or prevent us, in a sense, from losing something dear, something meaningful from our past or our present. You might find the strength to get through the day by some fantasy life you keep under your hat: you are James Bond in the Aston Martin, or in the famous white Lotus Esprit that becomes a submarine; maybe you are a dashing RAF pilot in your Morgan and any time now you will meet a lover to share your wine and lunch with. In short, the car can and often is our statement to the world, "This is me!" and it makes me happy or confident or reminds me of . . . .

This gorgeous Aston DB2 has haunted my garage for many years!

~

Choosing the Right Car

Perhaps no other choice hereafter makes much difference if you goof the first one! A bad choice of car is like a bad marriage: here you are unhappy, now that you are together and let me tell you "sickness" is somewhere on the near horizon! So going to all the trouble and expense to resurrect a car which does not "do it" for you will be a burden . . . . Take your time, read this book and read all you can on ALL the British sports cars you have ever thought might be "the one." There is so much "hidden" information: a fellow or damsel dashing down the road in a Morgan might be making your knees weak, but did you know they have a rather large part of their structure composed of wood?! Yes, and if it happens that powder post beetles are a regular nuisance around your property, then this might not be the car for you . . . . Perhaps reliability is very high on your list and a cross-country drive is part and parcel to the dream. Then a lot of thought needs to go into roadside support in the—heaven forbid—event of a failure, so maybe any car you choose should have suppliers able to ship something overnight? Many of you will not necessarily be able to sort out some of the more complicated failures which might occur, so a network of enthusiasts is a huge benefit. Most of the national car clubs publish a list of members across the country who will be willing to lend either special tools and technical support or a place to store the car till parts can be found. I myself have provided this service and helped some enthusiasts traveling long distance in an antique Lotus.

Try to envision the reality of how you would use your car. Reality is a good bit different from most people's dreams. The only times most collector cars poke their nose out into the sun is . . . well, when it's sunny. Most never see water that is not intentionally sprayed on them from a hose. Heaven forbid it should rain on them and actually need those wiper blades you spent $$$ on and had shipped from England. Never mind the huge bucks you spent to replace the wiper switch and/or motor! (more on purchasing from England later) . . . . No it seems that, in spite of all good and I do mean GOOD intentions, we tend to drive them about 1/80th of the time we thought! So keep this in mind and knowing this will perhaps change what car you decide on. On the other hand, I do know a small number of enthusiasts who drive the cars in all weathers and at all times of the year. They are numbering fewer every year as values rise and fears of accident damage weigh on our consciences (see my section on insurance and crashes), but some still brave the Buicks and keep the road hot . . . and I applaud them! Those people really know the dream and live it too. I bought my cars to drive and you should too!

So where do you find this dream car if the local club can't help and the national club has no suitable car for sale? *Hemmings Motor News* is truly the "bible of the old car hobby" and a pleasure to read. It covers ads for anything the car nut could desire; there's even a real estate section with car-oriented houses for collectors!

Look at Me!

Yes, you look good in that (insert car of choice here)! Like the growing majority of auction results watchers, are you inclined to choose originality and patina over fresh paint and soft new upholstery? Is it the color of your dreams or maybe not and you live with it? Maybe you committed the faux pas of a color change? What matters for most is "does it look . . . right?" Even though it might not be perfect preservation to alter the color, it still is your car (we hope) and it has to suit you and your vision, and, therefore, your statement to the world.

Saving a Thing of Beauty

There is a fantastic article by Peter Egan where he tries to explain his

attraction to old stuff. . . . I for one have always been drawn to things that
have stood the test of time (or perhaps laid quietly as it passed). I chuckle
at the common car magazines as they praise the latest plastic fantastic—
their covers proclaiming the "Three modes of ankle scratcher" not available on the past year's model (pity those poor buggers with only the two
modes!) now available in all markets (see dealer for details and a good
fleecing!) . . . . Remember that today's latest greatest . . . is tomorrow's
resident of the scrapyard! With the only exceptions being cars whose
prices look like overseas phone numbers and the few remaining low volume
manufacturers that you can actually ring up on the phone . . . , no collector cars have been produced since the seventies. Now before you knock
over your tea rushing to the computer to give me a good thrashing as to
why your '99 Supposoblob S3 fits rightly into the rear of the aforementioned categories, let me clarify, and this may come as a shock to many
an automotive neophyte (please read "enthusiast" here for the sake of my
inbox). Having spent my life keeping classics and other alleged automo-
biles running, I know what it takes in the design of things mechanical for
a machine to live many times the manufacturer's warranty (the expected
length of time the owner will not need to be on a first name basis with the
service department) and it is not, I repeat NOT . . . shock and awe here
. . . wait, here it comes . . . PLASTIC! This product, as wonderful as it
is for junior's version of daddy's car, should not be carrying too much in
the way of critical duty with the twirly bits under the bonnet! The second
most damning reason why mommie's grocery getter will be smelted down
long before you need a second valve job on your 1955 Godshespurty is
electronics! (And they are largely what? . . . Plastic!) Bursting plastic coolant pipes and radiators, shattering latches, razor sharp crumbling wiring
connectors go so nicely with failure in modules that run everything from
the ignition to memory seats (I can remember my own seat settings thank
you! No $500 module required.) These electronic devils with dubious life
spans are the scourge of the would-be merry motorist of today and thankfully not present in the 4-wheeled objects of my affections! (although some
foolhardy blighters actually install them on purpose in old classics, no doubt
to create an exciting element of unreliability, perhaps the chance that the

lightning storm in the distributor going dark like a passed thundershower gives them a thrill!).

~

Restoring Ethics

How many of us know of a classic car sitting in the garage of an acquaintance who claims he will restore that beauty "someday," only to see the once easy restoration deteriorate to the point of being unrealistic?

All classic machines must be used in the manner they were intended!! Sitting is damaging in so many ways that are not commonly understood! Grandma's old china will live forever in the cabinet unused but not so a complicated machine like a car!! It is very much like a human being in that it needs exercise to keep it healthy. The antifreeze turns to a corrosive, the oil forms a layer of acid, the convertible top fluids can turn to jell, and the brake fluid absorbs moisture and corrodes the brakes from the inside out! The oil seals dry out, leather seats mold and paint left covered with dust gets etched and scratched, tires dry rot. (Let's not even talk about what happens in your fuel system.) I am not suggesting you take out a second mortgage and do a Pebble Beach Concours but instead to focus on a realistic goal of driving the classic that inspired you. If it's not the one already in the garage, then go get the one you really want now and drive it (life is too short for boring cars); if it is the one in the garage, then let's get it going and enjoy it! Many of us are a little too romantic and a little unrealistic about our love of cars, so we tend to buy too many (and spread ourselves too thin) of the beauties which made our hearts flutter or made noises that make cows go dry and windows rattle . . . . Whatever brought you to the hobby, the real satisfaction comes in driving, in talking to others about this beauty of yours. Trying to restore too many cars can stop a restoration of any one of them from actually happening.

Consider again your acquaintance who is sitting on unused cars (the ones without current tags). This practice hurts the hobby in a number of ways I suspect they don't realize. Without even considering how this keeps the cars out of the hands of enthusiasts who would actually use them, doing so also increases the rarity and hence the price of the cars. Further, cars not in use don't consume parts, and manufacturers aren't going to make parts they don't sell, so the parts become more rare and expensive as the supply dwindles, or the quality lessens as they are now made in the Far East or just not at all!! So, five years from now when you do take the tarp off the poor captive beauty, the parts may not be there for YOU either!!

So if you are still not convinced enough to grab a wrench, then sell your classic to someone who will! Think about what you drove today: was it exciting? did you see another classic on the road?? Let's see them on the road! And let's be that cool person everyone's admiring!

~

Restoration or Desecration?

My Webster says . . . Restoration: "the act or process of returning something to its original condition."

In the auto trade the term "Restoration" is grossly misused! It is the norm for an ad in *Hemmings* or *Collector Car Trader* to describe a car as "restored," when, in fact, it has been so heavily modified that it is no longer of interest to a serious collector; it has, in fact, been "Desecrated"!

I have been along as advisor on "restorations" so badly damaging the car as to have to go sit in the rental we picked up at the airport, steaming with indignation that some heathen has robbed us of another fine potential beauty (now with engine swap and 50 lbs of Bondo . . .) while the prospect bids his adieus as we beat a hasty retreat, making room for a less-educated buyer!

A fine automobile having been designed, built, tested and then used for years and admired until it becomes "tired" should be "Restored" (as per the definition in *Webster*), not subjected to the ill-advised modifications of some "genius" working alone who thinks himself more capable than the entire staff of a major motor car manufacturing firm (and he always seems to be retired from some trade other than cars . . . .)! It's not only the owners' failure to understand; often they are led astray by magazines about "Restoration" and ads for modifications . . . . If those ads for improved shifting, better highway mileage and brighter headlights really attract you, then go get the Honda you wanted and leave the classics to someone who will take care of them properly . . . . Please!

~

It's in My Blood

Is it possible that Castrol could be the thick and gooey that my heart pumps? And is it possible also, as claimed by some of my closest friends, that when cut, I bleed yellow and green (the colors on the Lotus nose badge) ?! Now that I ponder all the times I've been cut, stabbed, abraded and otherwise injured while my hands were deep in the entrails of some very cool but temporarily ill chariot of charm, no doubt I do have every type of automotive fluid coursing through my veins; perhaps in the event of a heart attack, they will substitute a set of jumper cables for the defibrillator and 20W50 (in summer) instead of plasma?

But in all seriousness (or as much seriousness as is available in this text), there must be some reason we are like this (many chuckles here and the raised eyebrows of our better halves) . . . . so maybe it was an episode of *The Avengers* where Ms. Peel speeds by the camera in her Lotus or perhaps it was Mr. Steed? (no reflection on your sexual orientation). Maybe it was some scene in a movie where that which now stands in your driveway did first show itself? However the dream came to be, or is now forming from the mist, it likely feels more like a need than a desire! The practice with most Americans is to claim a hyphenated origin "Irish-American," "Italian-American," etcetera, and you might justify your Alvis sports car thusly, "Alvis-American." Perhaps you justify your BRG HRG some other way: " My Father had one," "I rode in one in college and always cherished those days" (seems to me that connecting to days past is one of the larger rationalization methods). It is undeniable that those cars at the top of the value scale can be simply objects of such divine beauty they are pieces of art; we all know that the E type coupe was displayed in New York at the museum of modern art! Many years ago a dear friend brought me a photograph he took through someone's window in Amsterdam. The living room had a early Lotus Élan set up so one could look at the car or sit in it and watch TV! Many machines that don't have to cost 6 or 7 figures qualify for this sort of adoration. For many years . . . in my library . . . I had a 1967 Triumph motorcycle I had restored! Even now in my living room is a British Seagull outboard motor (perhaps I shouldn't tell you these things?). However you rationalize your absolute need to have that car, I am here to be your support group, your shoulder to lean a bumper on, a helping hand for left hand or right hand drive!

Being interviewed by Keith Martin at the Kiawah Island Motoring retreat

Stewards of History

But you must be a steward of this piece of history that you now own. If not, this is my chance to yell at you through my keyboard, for it is my belief that you . . . yes, you! . . . are no doubt making terrible mistakes! Now heed this my children—the call to righteousness: "what is not right is wrong!" And ye who stray from the path shall be damned by . . . Christies, Mecum, Barrett Jackson, and the entire free market in general! Most heinous be the color changes and those who . . . (gasp!) . . . change the engines (oh how I shudder!). A CD player might be excused by the complacent but not I, for I have seen the light (or perhaps the auction results)!

Ok, really, . . . no matter how deep your car is underground on the Ol' totem pole . . . get a heritage certificate from whatever body officiates your chosen marque and stick to it! The only exceptions are period accessories and options which might have been available from the manufacturer. There is nothing to be gained—and plenty to be lost—in the driving experience by even the most common mods, such as wider tires. This, by example, spoils the steering on vintage cars: it ruins the turn in on Lotus Cortinas by example and cracks the Burman steering boxes on others. Really . . . , need I say more?! Delrin and other hard bushes on A arms might give more "road feel" but at the same time transmit more shock and stress to the frame and ye butt that rides in it!

Tracey and Bruce at an irresistible photo opportunity in the Charleston low country.

SECTION 2:

THE JOYS

Family, Friends and Lovers!

Blood is thicker than water, but somewhat less viscous than oil . . . . Often, but not as often as I would like . . . cars are passed on to the children. Fond memories of the parents driving you around in that very same car that you now pilot must be the greatest treasure for the collector! I have numerous clients in this hallowed category and try to keep pictures of them on the shop walls as examples of what "should be," and my favorite such picture is of Millie Horton. She comes up in my phone as "Millie Horton Bentley" if that gives you any clue. In fact, it would be appropriate if that were her "Christian name." This adorable woman and her charming husband Tom are the lucky owners of her mother and father's 1953 Bentley R-Type and, unlike most people, she uses it; not in rain of course, but on every occasion that could even loosely be considered appropriate, there she is, in acres of leather, making the world a better, prettier place to be!

Millie Horton and I driving onto the green to accept her award at the KIMR

I have another client who also inherited the family cars. He and his sister were given the cars when they graduated college; the daughter was given the Bentley (a different girl this time) and the son got the MGTD . . . and both still have them! Heart-warming stuff that!

It's likely if you still get "up" in the morning, you might also get "up" at the sight of not only your 1964 Smoothashell but also a fetching figure of the opposite sex. Then, as any red-blooded car lover might think, a cozy two seater is just the thing for the intimacy two might desire (four seaters are for the more adventuresome and/or unattached, but no need to discuss that in front of the kids). Few among us don't have some warm (perhaps hot) memories of some excursion on wheels and "running out of gas" or "parking," and while all this is swimming in your mind (naughty you!), consider how much more special a memory it is when made in an MG TC than in a Vega! (My apologies, of course, to those of you possibly conceived in lesser vessels of passion!). So find a quiet spot, turn on that AM radio and maybe they're playing a little Burt Jumpinback . . . oh, the memories . . . .

It's not only our significant others that ride along—or when we are feeling generous get a chance to drive. Often, it's our best buddies or perhaps the only guy that will talk to you (you do have a reputation for droning on about car stuff . . .)! We seem to enjoy sharing our love of cars with anyone even slightly inclined to listen to our preaching: poor cousin Frank when visiting at Christmas becomes your captive audience in the TVR as you carry on about the virtues of Yokohama tires and you soon have him convinced that one of those cars from Blackpool will grace his garage when the house, belonging to recently passed Auntie Bertha, gets sold! Whatever the reason for your choice or circumstances that brought you here, now that your trusty steed awaits . . . .

~

No two communicate better than Michele and her Super Seven!

Drive!

I am no longer shocked at how many alleged enthusiasts do not use their cars as much as they planned or envisioned when they bought them. I hear all the great ideas of crossing the country and "driving till the wheels fall off," and, the next thing you know, it's being towed into my shop to have the old gas drained out and a new battery because they didn't run it last year! . . . so let's examine a few ironies. First, the "I'm afraid to drive it out of town" quote, often uttered by someone who has done a thousand local miles last year, never once dialing me or AAA ! "Hey there!" You could have gone to Miami and back! Highway miles are much less stressful than the stop and go you do around town. Just ask John Scott; he has driven his immaculate Jaguar MK2 up and down the east coast from Vermont to Charleston, S. C. and beyond (of course, it is rather comfy in that car . . .) and, even if you do break down in some fashion, the adventure factor will give you another story to tell! My friend and Morgan owner John

Thompson loves the way when he stops to correct some small malady, scores of interested people stop to see the car and perhaps help; he sees the whole experience as opportunity! Then there's the "It might rain" excuse, often uttered by the same guy who spends over an hour washing said same rolling prisspot! I am also amazed by people who won't drive in anything colder than 55 degrees and have never turned on the heater!

However, not everyone hides in the garage waiting for the perfect day! Dennis Oldland, my longtime friend and rabid British car enthusiast, is one of those rare individuals who can do—and does—almost all of the work on his own car (thankfully, he has me do the deep engine work or I'd be left out entirely!) He has amazed me for years doing restorations of several Lotus cars and a 1967 E type partly in my shop and then . . . on the road he goes, racking up miles at a rate similar to me! or more! Cold of winter, heat of summer—no problem; he's out there! I hope you are so lucky to be a Dennis, but if you're not, the game is still on . . . keep reading!

~

What to Put in the Boot

Once you have determined that you *will* drive that cherished chariot, rumbler, love machine, be sure you have a well-stocked boot. Do I have suggestions for this, you query? You bet your balaclava I do, so take notes—grab your Waterman fountain pen or your quill and well, let's get started!

Beginning with the smaller cars and focusing on what every car needs in her cubby or boot, the motoring enthusiast will no doubt find it comforting to don a proper cap. I have noted recently some fine choices: a Balmoral or flat cap certainly gives an air of authenticity to the driver of a Morgan, for instance, and Holden's in the UK sells some quite fetching Ladies motoring hats (lovely image that). A beret, although not typically associated with the Brits, does give the impression there might have been a recent trip across the Channel or drive down the Champs Elysées! Those of us inclined towards the Lotus Seven or Morgan Three wheeler might be better presented in a leather flying helmet (and they go so well with the classic bomber jacket). All that fluffy wool around the edges truly giving the image of "Derring do"!

Scarves are a must for both the Ladies and Gentlemen but tie them short so as not to go the way of Isadora Duncan!

No proper Gentleman or Lady should grasp the wheel without the appropriate gloves. String backs are by far the most correct although there are many good leather gloves for motoring (thin ones for better feel if it's not too cold . . .).

Perhaps the sun reflections from your gleaming bonnet are too much to bear? No doubt you have considered shading your peepers. So important to better see the oncoming blighter in a Buick who is more intent on texting than turning. Also handy for taking note unnoticed in the event of attractive roadside scenery. The racer types will, of course, go for the Halcyon goggles with tinted lenses (again very good with the bomber jacket and leather helmet).

Lap blankets are a most welcome advantage, for it seems that strangely our right little rides have woefully inadequate heaters or "Fug stirrers" as properly called. More often than not, they produce somewhat less warmth than a mouse breathing on your knee and any cooling of one's lady's body might also cool her ardeure . . . . Upon arrival at that destination afar, your famished companion can now recline comfortably while you twirl your corkscrew like a seasoned sommelier.

Note, the Welsh make absolutely the finest motoring/picnic blankets. The basket itself (you didn't think I would omit the very holy grail of all motoring accessories, did you?!) should contain all manner of accoutrement necessary for a lunch among the well bred; a mellon baller is going too far, but at least two types of spoons are de rigueur! Napkins should match at least a little bit of the classical patterns found on one's kilt (you do have a kilt don't you . . . ?) Wedgewood is perfect and Waterford crystal also separates one from the groveling masses at any decent polo match!

Umbrellas that suit your lady should be left to her choosing as there is no possibility of your understanding how to match them to her attire much less her mood! Opera glasses or perhaps a brass telescope for admiring the scenery (careful at the beach lest your lady take the aforementioned umbrella to your cap a time or two)!

And now on to the larger conveyances of correctness . . . Bentleys, Rolls and Range Rovers have the capacity for a proper table and chairs as well as other necessities one might find it difficult to convey in an MG Midget such as the ice bucket, coolers, shooting sticks, clays and ammunition, Polo clubs and inflatables for the beach.

Musical instruments can be much the advantage when serenading your lovely although not while driving unless of course you are adept with a Kazoo.

Well, there you have it! Now pump in the petrol and grab that bottle of Chateau de Huile and off you go.

~

Car Shows

The Lotus owners gathering, Biltmore in Asheville, N.C.

Ah, the sight of rows upon rows of gleaming Healeys and TR3s and all the other joys of internal combustion! Oh how I do love a car show, leaning in and seeing all those lovely dashboards and all the other pleasures of a petrol and Tea nature. Here is where most of us realize our dreams, the place where we see for the first time (those new to this stuff anyway) those rolling dream machines that we simply must have. Unfortunately, those with shallow pockets might have to let go of that which they previously thought to be their "holy grail" car in order to get the one they now know to be the perfect ride! This is the best way to really find out what the cars look like, and owners are all too eager in most cases to help you along in acquiring the same type of car as they find dear. Most everyone is a member of at least one national owners group and one local enthusiast group. Within the pages of club newsletters is often the best place to find a car or the elusive part that has left you driving the grocery getter. Talk to the owners at events, so let's have a look at . . .

Clubs (support groups)

With Michele at the Retromobile in Paris - should be on everyone's bucket list....

Clubs are an absolute gift! We often sit in a circle; everyone gets a turn to stand up, state his name and explain how he came to this point. There is always a great deal of good advice, sometimes hugs, and we all know we can depend on each other to get us through and help us with the steps . . . ahhh, I feel better already!

For a small fee, often the largest clubs will offer a certificate of origin with the original build details for your car and sometimes even the original purchaser's name. Many clubs undertake the special manufacture of obsolete parts and can often be the only source worldwide! They very often have a list of experts who have dealt with the particular problems of your chosen marque and have discovered solutions that your mechanic (myself included) have no knowledge of. Were it not for the many fantastic clubs, we would not have the many delightful events and forums, so useful and fun! Look online or interview people you meet locally about the best group. I have many times walked up to complete strangers in a grocery store parking lot, for instance, to chat about the car they are driving (it's an addiction!) and often they are pleased and amazed to find out about the local clubs and events! Seems very few owners of classics are snobs or Scrooges although there have been a few memorable individuals who should perhaps no longer contribute to the gene pool . . . . As far as finding your national or local group, the internet has been an absolute boon. Here you can communicate with the HRG world club about the low slung chassis piece you are missing or find the local machine shop that "lives and breathes" old cars and can make the part you need or fix the one you have! Find your club and get involved at whatever level you can (As you might guess, I try to contribute a little mechanical knowledge to members here and write the occasional article for the newsletter.)

Most local level clubs also support some kind of charity through contributions generated by their car shows, so there's one more good reason, at the very least, to go to the shows! Our fantastic local club here is The British Car Club of Charleston and what a support group it is. If you are, say, feeling dismal about your tendency to spend more than your income on your car, someone in the group might have a brilliant idea, such as a second job, embezzling or perhaps a straightforward bank heist to support the habit! Really a jolly lot they are, and they organize technical seminars and socials all year long. You would be hard pressed to find a better car club!

So, what about that chassis part for your HRG?; better move on to . . .

~

Machine Shops . . .

Are by nature a gathering of "gear heads." Generally speaking, any machine shop will have grown out of a guy or group that loves cars and just can't get enough of the hobby. The best shops will usually be agonizingly slow due to huge backlogs. Think about it: if a shop is not busy is that because the machinist is so good?

It's very likely, unless you buy a finished car, that at some point you will need to visit those guys. Any serious engine rebuild will be better done using the expensive precision tools the machine shop has and with their experienced hands making the worn bits like new again! When the parts are back from the machine shop, then the same logic applies to Mechanics . . . .

Mechanics are a special breed; it is said that they are "parts guys gone mad." There are basically two types of mechanics "good" and "parts changers." Good mechanics spend a bit more time thinking about a problem before tackling it and are universally in demand. Their shops are slow and expensive, so you wonder, "why does everyone go there?" Well, there are a lot of dynamics here: would you go to the cheapest brain surgeon? the cheapest carpenter? In short, if you love your car, it seems that you would prefer that it actually get fixed rather than keep paying for the same repair over and over by a guy who throws all the wrong parts at it. Also important to note is that modern reproduction parts are almost all inferior to original parts: that's right, the brand new widget you bought is junk compared to the 40-year-old one in the car. Alas, the one in the car is dead and you have no choice do you? . . . or do you?! Maybe the only way to get the part is to find it "NOS," an acronym for "New Old Stock." The most expensive way to maintain your car? Maybe not. Actually, it's cheaper in most cases to fix the car once rather than three times . . . such as often occurs with "rebuilt" parts. The quality of rebuilt parts varies dramatically, somewhere between almost as good as NOS and not good enough to bother installing! Case in point, recently a client with an 80's Jag had a failed starter. He nearly gave birth to twins when I told him the cost and time frame from my normal supplier. When we cleaned up the mess from his initial shock and convulsions, he insisted that we use the local chain and they must be fine because "they are guaranteed for life!" and are half the price! He muttered something derogatory about me as I sent him to said chain to purchase said starter. I explained that I would not warranty his "provided" part and bolted it on in his presence . . . . It was no good . . . , wouldn't even turn once. I removed it—the "brand new rebuilt"—and sent him back. The next day they got him another and it did work, but he threw a fit when I charged him for two R&R (remove and replace) fees: I knew I had done the job twice, but he apparently forgot our conversation about warranty. I took pity (stupidly) and reduced my bill. The Jag returned a week later on the back of a wrecker, the owner more than willing to pay for my warranted product and another labor charge (something about being stranded with guests in the rain . . .)!

Alas, even a good mechanic can be befuddled; it's a terrible feeling for a mechanic, very different from being confused about all the beers on tap at the local. This is serious business for a guy who makes his living by a crystal ball and being able to see through steel panels. Our special ocular implants allow us to see the paths of electrons and where breaks are, in wires under carpets and in failed switches . . . (actually, that's a fantasy; we don't really do that stuff). We learn from experience the likely points of failure and the probability factors for different types of failures, and, as a result of increasing age (the vehicles that is!) and the attempts by other would-be technicians, the failures often change in nature. I recently found another shop had accidentally put a screw through a wire in an attempt at repair. Rather than simply find what they had done wrong, they ran a new wire, and me being me . . . I could not stomach an incorrectly colored wire that clearly was not original . . . . Three hours later, I had removed half the interior before I found it. After all that, and all back together, nothing looks different, but I knew it was right and the owner was thrilled (he thinks like I do, " poor guy"!)

~

The Art of Not Needing a Mechanic (or lots of parts!)

The cost of everything with our cars being either a bit expensive or too much for the coffers to cough . . . most of us would prefer that our rides continue on without too much in the repair budget! Here are some tips: Firstly, a big difference between long-term success and frequent failure is the unbelievably simple act of checking one's fluids—not that gin and tonic; I meant the car's fluids. Letting the oil run low enough to see the result in the oil pressure gauge—or worse yet, an idiot light—is certain to do horrible damage. Even if everything seems fine and you topped it up again, you have done damage! Coolant a little low doesn't sound too bad . . . wrong! Some cars have the thermostat very high on the engine and an air bubble in the thermostat housing can actually prevent the device from opening, followed by a potentially blown head gasket or worse! It is common for me to find low brake fluid on cars with or without warning lights (people tend to ignore those pesky little things even lit in red!). This can be a game changer, as in "out of the game"! Prior to 1968, brakes were "single circuit" and when the fluid gets so low as to draw in a bit of air . . . then the car in front of you will slow you down! In the interest of saving money on engine repair, I have developed an engine protection system for early Aston Martin engines; however, in early trials the shop dog was terribly difficult to shut off once the alarm had started. Perhaps a Corgi was not the right choice (the Queen keeps them) . . . maybe a Bulldog? So, if you do nothing else in the way of maintenance, please keep the fluids full! I've never tried to calculate it, but the failures resulting in towing are very high for lost fluids, when it would have been possible to keep using the car and, at your leisure, schedule a visit to see why that spot keeps growing under the car and friends make you park on the street!

~

Noises

The average-aged British car still galloping along merrily will have something of a cacophony of noises that most owners have grown used to. This may or may not be a good thing! Klunk from the drive line should not be ignored: perhaps the klunk occurs when getting on and off the throttle. Could be a universal joint dreaming of a new roadside home! Could be a motor mount and soon your engine will literally try to lie on her side for a much-needed rest! Bump and bang sounds, when going over rough surfaces and such, are often shocks or the bushings they mount in. When left to their own devices, they can do damage to the places where they mount. I have straightened many a Jaguar from this ignored malady! Rattles often result from things simply being loose and a good day of poking and prodding, tightening in the vicinity of the noise with screwdrivers, wrenches and WD40 will find or cure the trouble. Keep in mind that in cars, noises can be far from where you think they are, so enlist a friend to listen as well so you can concentrate on driving . . . good thinking there! . . . and speaking of thinking . . .

~

Psychology

Well, I had to come to this part at some point, so might as well give you the good and bad news right away rather than at the end of the book, so if you've not already been "committed" but you peek carefully out the curtains now and again in fear of the guys carrying very very long-sleeved jackets intent on putting one on you, then make sure you are committed!, (yes, it was auntie that alerted them to your clearly mad plot to sell her house and buy a TVR), (couldn't wait till she "passed" could you?)

"The Good," in general the sort of person who is a long term British car collector/owner, tends to be a bit more relaxed! (Rare is the teetotaler in this group!) And going nicely with the relaxed moods, boat ownership, past or present, is also quite common in the crowd concerned (although mostly when living near water . . . boat ownership in the desert will bring on one of those long sleeve jackets I mentioned!) Also a positive is that British car collectors are generally a gregarious lot—fun to be with! As much of our time as is absorbed with this hobby, it is quite amazing, but common, that other hobbies accompany that of British car ownership! I once met a fellow with an MG TC who built harpsichords!—there are many hidden talents within the mind inclined to drive a car that leaks so much oil out below and rain in from above!

The Bad news . . . Well there isn't any . . . (it is my book you know!)

~

Autocrossing

Now many of you who are a bit less lucky might believe auto crossing to be something Catholic and involving oily rosary beads, although many of us have prayed on the roadside either in genuine hope or using "sailors prayers" to loosen some stuck lug nut or what have you. This is not the case; autocrossing is, in fact, a method of turning bravado into shame as it turns out you are actually not Fangio and simply never got your chance but are a wee bit slower than you believed, and in this we find a perfect way to know beyond a shadow of a doubt what you and your mount are really capable of ! I highly recommend the practice though not necessarily for all cars: many of the collector's items should not be run too hard and the stresses such as oil surge and the obvious strains on suspension components might unseat you till your favored repair facility has deeply raided your checkbook! If your chosen car was originally deeply in the "sports" categories, then by all means you should give it a try and the fact is that it's better to discover a potential weak point in the company of enthusiasts than to be in the wilds one night and have not so successfully avoided a problem when you discover you really should have had that klunk noise checked!

My own brother had decided that certainly he was one of those "born drivers" and had to have absolutely the fastest possible car and without much hesitation jumped into the fray with the most expensive auto cross project we could dream up, a Lotus Europa TC. We picked up the car in Georgia as a rebuildable project; he lavished the cash on it and I lavished the mechanical labors and know-how on it. He seemed totally invincible! He ran "class A street prepared" and after three years at it had no other choice but to penny up and get a tow rig and trailer. It was go big time or get out, so he got out. It's an expensive hobby and, having satisfied himself that he really was a born driver, he moved on and the car went to Hayes Harris at Wirewheel in Florida, a specialist in buying and selling Lotus. I was sad to see it go. That car proved not only that Dan was a "born driver," but that I could build them to go fast! I have built and improved quite a few cars to autocross, and it's always a pleasure to see the excitement people get from the experience!

~

Vintage Racing

For those of you whose passions might be of the faster variety, beware that your wallet might run hotter than your engine, but if you choose to go the road only traveled by the likes of Nuvolarie, then read on! There are plenty of ways to take objects of beauty out on the track! Remember that most insurances prohibit this type of driving, but you can buy track-day insurance for when the mood strikes you! So, you have your racing tyres, (that's the Queen's English for "tires"!) the Webers are tuned to perfection and you dialed in the camber perfectly to handle this circuit—are you ready? If yes, then no doubt you are going to create memories not unlike alluded to in a previous chapter in this book! There are few things one can do that compare with the feel of real competition on a real track but take care not to swap paint as the focus of this book, and I assume you, is the preservation of a cherished collector car. It is generally accepted that vintage racing is not going to be too dangerous for car or driver, and most organizations will quickly ban you from their events if there is any tendency whatsoever for your driving to be less than very careful! Join a vintage or historic racing association and do a lot of drivers' schools before trying this! (Everyone should do a drivers' school with a trained instructor, whether you plan to autocross or not!)

~

The Younger Generations

I'm often in discussions where it is suggested that the young people will have no interest in cars and the end draws nigh! "Not so, say I." How would you explain the interest in Model A cars, the London-to-Brighton run, etc.? Those certainly weren't the cars they saw as teenagers or in college. By that measure then, if you were a teenager longing for a 1929 Model A, you are how old . . . ? No, in fact, it seems that I have always had about the same number of teenagers who enjoy visiting the shop and who save their money for a classic they can afford. What is needed is just to expose them to the hobby. Take that nephew with the peculiar piercings for a pleasant ride (yes, he's horridly ugly but there could be potential under the ol' hat rack!) As might be expected, my own son has fallen in with this group known as "gear heads" and, sooner than his dad is ready, he'll be wheeling around in his series 1 Lotus Europa! His friends also seem to be afflicted with cars although generally marques much less deserving of devotion . . . . "The wrench doesn't fall far from the toolbox" as they say!

SECTION 3:

REALITY

Paying for It!

"If you have to ask then you can't afford it!" I've heard that quote used in garages for many years, but it really isn't true . . . . It makes sense to get an idea what the mechanic thinks it will cost to do a repair or restore a system, but don't think it gospel; no one can really know what it will cost until it's done. Case in point, a water pump recently. The job was quoted for "X" dollars and all was going well, but that bottom bolt stripped out and it took twice as long to fix that hole as the entire rest of the job! In general, if someone is insistent on having a firm quote, then I just "sky-ball" them (that's a really high quote) so if it all goes wrong, I don't have to call them and hear all that crying about "you said"! Anyone with car sense knows things can be harder to fix than at first glance!

~

Rose-colored Glasses

Seems there are a lot of those rose glasses on bed stands atop the latest *Hemmings* . . . . I know of many disassembled cars in garages that were going to be done in a summer. Now 10 years or more later, the parts are scattered and the time is no longer available. I also am guilty of thinking how this project or that will take only a fraction of what it really will . . . . The trick here is to not do it! Yup, it's easier to keep the peace at home if you just give up and sell it as a project and buy Lovey the car she wanted in running condition . . . ! If that won't get it, then some delegation of authority might be in order: have a pro do the motor and a pro do the body and you trim back your duties to trim! There will be plenty of stuff you didn't think about to stop you in your tracks later, so you can start the cycle all over again . . . but you'll be closer!

~

Storage

The FIRST thing to do in the collector car hobby is establish proper storage. There's no point in having a fabulous car and parking it under a beach house with so much salt film on the glass you can't see out. Any storage should be dry and dark. I've seen plenty of carport-stored cars with all the paint faded on one side. Storage is an area you really have to budget big for! I am lucky that I am in the biz and keep my cars covered in my shop or at friends' shops.

Your storage area should also be well organized to hold and be able to find all those little things one must have that go with maintenance and restoration, not just wax and Armor All but oil and filters, spare fan belts etc. . . . . A solid work bench will greatly enhance your restoration experience; getting all these things in order is just as important as buying the car!

Covers that breathe are a good idea and please don't stack things on cars. After that pile of light boxes hits the ceiling, the combined weight now has your bonnet turned into a bowl!,and who's gonna just jump on that project if it's a project just to unearth it . . . . Please don't make things worse (she's already mad at you for the coffee this morning!)

~

Displaying Your Beauty

We love a good movie or concert and certainly a good car show. Alas, they can be a bit few and far between. Despair not; the next best thing and a huge joy is to turn your garage into a shrine dedicated to your very cool car. Anything you can find from that year might look great around the shop/garage/bar/museum . . . bedroom! Yes, I have seen a loft-over design where an enthusiastic fellow could be from slumber to Sunbeam Tiger in steps! Posters with appropriate track lighting don't really cost that much. Track lighting can highlight the latest detailing taking place under the bonnet as well! Music is a must—perhaps the stereo can be right there next to the refrigerator (all this happy imagery is making me thirsty!) A glas display cabinet was in one of my garages, and I filled it with knick-knacks from the trade and all those trophies one collects (The mantle collapse in the house should tell you to do something!) Car covers can be rolled back during visitors' hours. A friend of mine with a large collection likes to lift only a corner of each cover, revealing just a little of the joy hidden beneath! He calls it the "raised skirt technique" and a small fee is charged, such as a good adult beverage (see how profitable this book is!) A dart board is good so long as the flight path is taken into its due consideration! Stacks of old car magazines are a delight for all the gear-heads; comfy chairs are good, and bar stools allow easy moving to view different angles!

~

Dealing with Shops (knowing who your friends are)

Unless you are already a brilliant mechanic, you will, at some point, find repair shops necessary. The automotive trade has a terrible reputation and with very good reason: competent mechanics or technicians, as they like to call themselves nowadays, are few and far between. The fact is that the repair end of the industry does not attract the Ivy League. Sorry, but the more likely scenario is it's a guy who finished high school (maybe) with some notable exceptions, but, nonetheless, the people in the business of replacing the alternator on your 2003 "Where's-the-groceries" don't really have "factory training," and all those other things sewn onto the uniform might not be as helpful as you would like in preparing Mr. Wrenchright to do battle under your bonnet! So forget the shops where modern cars go and do yourself a favor; find the specialist on your specific make and model. It will, in the long run, save you a fortune . . . unless they are just out to pose as brilliant in order to empty your wallet.

Rather than get myself a bunch of threats from these guys, I will simply suggest that you talk to several people who use the garages you locate before trusting them with your little beauty. The days have long passed since the corner garage could competently repair anything on wheels that chose to poke in the roll-up door. Now cars are a totally different ball game and the repairs on our old cars are so foreign (no pun intended) to the present day "technician" that he's totally out of place. He'll find no OBD2 plug under the dash (that's the place on a modern car where one plugs in the mechanic's handheld computer that talks to your car's commuter; it's kinda like your car going to a therapist . . .) and possibly has never seen a side draft carburetor. If he can't hook up his laptop and reflash the software, it's you who will be pushing it onto the wrecker so it can be taken to a more capable shop . . . . The stories I will not print would bring tears to anyone who cares about his car. Just be sure to get several recommendations before leaving her, him, it there . . . .

~

Costs of Restoration or Repair

The truth about restoration in general is that on cars that were produced in "quantity," it is far far cheaper to buy one ready to go than to have one you found cheap, restored. The only time I break that rule is if the customer has a special attachment to that specific car—"it was Dad's" etc. In that case, you can see that finding another one just isn't going to do and spending roughly twice its finished value is what you should expect—perhaps even a bit more. All the different cars have unique things about them that make generalizing a bit risky; Lotus engines of the "twin cam" variety cost twice as much to overhaul as the same size MG B engine, and we're not talking frills here! Body work on some cars is comparatively inexpensive; many reproduction panels are available but some cars have to have every panel hand made . . . . That's not cheap! Most people seem to be clueless as to the cost of painting collector cars, too, laboring under the belief that Earl the paint guy will do a great job and a color change for $1500 . . . yeah right . . .

~

Random Misfire

Here's a classic example of the clueless owner and the reality of restoration and/or maintenance. Ok. Let's see . . . "Random misfire" and "misfire cylinder #11" . . . . Looks like you need the basic ignition service. "When would you like to do that?" "How much?" "Oh, about $4000." "That was a nasty fall; can I help you up, get some aspirin?" "Well, of course I can break it down" : 12 spark plugs at $40.91 each, 12 coils at $157.56 each, a manifold gasket set at $407.36 and around $900 labor . . . . "
"How often?" "Well, about every 25 or 30 thousand miles." "Perhaps you should sit down again, you look faint!"

What I'm trying to point out here is that for the people who, for instance, left the three-year-old Benz in the driveway this morning and drove the Suburban, it's possible to drive a spectacular car as your secondary "real car." Live a little! Sound expensive? Maybe you just need to rethink all the math! The above quote was for an Aston Martin, one of the most desirable cars in the world! Most people with that sort of car put fewer than 5000 miles a year on the car, so that's an every-5-years' experience, and, given the miles I've put on 12-cylinder Astons over my many years servicing them, I'd say that's a bargain! Here's some more perspective . . . Ferrari service schedules include a timing belt, drive belts, and a similar ignition service every 20,000 miles for about $1500 more on average! So here we have an Aston eating less than $1000 per year for service (not including oil changes) and a Ferrari eating a little more than a grand per annum. Ok, here comes the painful part: even the most boring modern rain car—a Buick or BMW—in your driveway is eating more in depreciation! The Ferrari is ticking up slowly and the Aston is bottomed out or losing a little for a couple more years.

So, you say you wouldn't want to park it at the grocery store for fear of a ding in the door? Are you really suggesting you wouldn't fix a ding in your Mercedes? your Tahoe? It's all the same: the body shop might bump up the cost of painting the door on your Rolls a bit but not that much . . . I'll grant you that truly exciting cars are not for everybody. Seeing yourself repeatedly during the day must be comforting—like lemmings swimming safely in the company of many others all the same, and the consideration of maintenance, being the same or even cheaper, might not outweigh the simplicity of swimming to the nearest service center instead of seeking out and waiting for an appointment (sometimes weeks away) at the specialist needed for an exciting car.

I know we have dogs and the need to carry Auntie for an airing from the oldies home once in a while, so a rain car is, I admit, a necessity for most of us. But that other car . . . you know the one . . . , live a little and have a dream car! It might actually cost less than your Lemming mobile!

~

The Difference between "New" and "Now" . . .

Back in the 90's I restored for myself a 1965 Lotus Élan S2; literally no two things were left touching each other! I personally rebuilt every part of the car and reassembled it from a sandblasted and re-seam welded frame up. Everything was loved on to the point that it was as much as possible a new car and it drove like it! I used it constantly for quite a few years with my only problems being a loose coil lead and an incident where I had knocked my clutch hose too close to the exhaust. When I sold the car (what a dumb move!), the fellow flew in from Texas and simply drove it home! So . . . wouldn't you like to use a (your favorite car here) every day. You can and should. It is the tendency of many a car nut to continuously restore cars and resell them, and almost always he will be forced to sell them at a loss, without counting his time. The trick is did he do a good job? It's one thing to hire a professional to restore a car for you (a very expensive thing!) but quite another to put your faith in the work of a guy that is not in the trade! Take heart, however! I have seen absolutely stunning restorations done in home garages; nothing seems to please the home guy more than doing for $20K what I would not be able to do in my shop for less than $60K. What he doesn't want to talk about is his divorce and the 2000 hours he spent, but that's not the issue. What I am suggesting is that you find him and buy his car (he might get hi wife back!) especially if you are the sort who "couldn't fix a sandwich." Another tremendous benefit of the "toss me the keys and I'm off" type of purchase is that you are at the car show WITH your car rather than it being scattered around half the country. However, it's also good to point out that because some home restorations tend to take so many years that the car is almost certainly stacked with boxes in the garage so deep the car disappears and friends tend to forget you have it, you might want to sell now, so someone will restore it. Then, you can go out and buy one ready to go! Also in professional shops it is not uncommon for a restoration to take a year for any car more complicated than an MG! So, you are going to restore that car, work your day job, and renovate the house . . . ? What are you? Superman?

~

Voices from the Past

We won't need a Ouija board for this, but eBay might be helpful? A large part of the joy of owning, restoring, and caring for these cars is the research into the original records for build sheets or the names of the owners, finding the elusive special order part available only for that car in that year, or just the right period picnic basket (the sky's the limit on the cost you can incur for accessories!). Collecting old car magazines, for one, is a delight, and if you are lucky, finding one with a picture of your favored car on the cover can be treasure! They are often filled with interesting things from the past not related to cars but giving the flavor of the period. Old magazines are very helpful in finding the voices of the past and hearing their message. Let me clarify for those who don't already scan the realm for these oracles. A period article can tell you what failures you might expect; it can tell you what the cars were really supposed to look like; and what the car's strong points were—much like collecting paintings, you would not want anything to be less than correct as this reduces the value of your investment and is an affront to history! Certainly we are all aware of the quote that "History is written by the victors," but this should not translate into changing the car to suit your desire if you have any concern for preserving history! If you are in the camp of less concern, read on and perhaps we can bring you to the path of righteousness!

Cost of Maintenance

Ok, this is really my arena. The cost of maintenance can make or break the joy we may or may not derive from our chosen chariot. This is where we have to say to ourselves "oops" or "this is heaven"! I have a reputation for being brutally honest and there is a method behind this madness. While many an educated business man will tell you, "the customer is always right," we all know that's crap! In almost every instance the customer knows little or nothing about what is needed; he is an enthusiast who has a good idea about the vision of what he or she wants. Whether or not it's realistic or wise, it is my job to advise him! If a customer wants something that does not make sense economically or is damaging to the historical value of a rare car, I tell them so. Last year a fellow with a perfectly presentable E coupe inquired after a partial restoration, including a color "adjustment." I knew from experience that the result would be a huge disappointment and be quite costly as well, so to his amazement I declined the work even though I had a restoration bay opening in a few weeks. Why would a guy in the "biz" turn down easy money? Simple logic: I would want the same wisdom passed on to me in an area I did not deeply understand! Plus, I routinely discourage restoring cars with excellent patina. There are plenty of nice restos out there but precious few original cars. They can be original only once! It is the speciality of a really good shop to leave a job as though "nothing had ever been disturbed," all the original appearance in place so that the only evidence of a repair is "the clean spot"! Not doing work that to my mind does not need doing allows the customer to make repairs that are truly needed, and, in the long run, this practice makes the car cheaper to own! Also as previously remarked, the good shops are always busy. don't need more work! So, you ask, "why not hire and build and grow?"

Simple logic: I am not in this position because the work coming out of my shop is often found wanting! I have in the past had a crew of mechanics, but chasing behind them and trying to get them as much interested in my moral point of view was taking about as much time as just doing it myself (I'm rather picky). The possibly surprising philosophy (remember the title?) of "I am working for the car not you" is difficult for many to understand, so to get these guys to always check behind themselves was never easy, and when I had, on all too frequent occasions, to "redo" jobs that came back, I eventually decided it made more sense to just go it alone. That makes for long hours and little free time. I wear a blue tooth so my hands can keep moving during the 20 to 50 phone calls a day! And while it's fresh in my thinker, you do realize that if you happen to be distracting me from working on "your" car and I am changing say . . . "brake parts," do you think we should change my focus right now, hmmm?

At the Lotus owners gathering in Florida and, as always, on the phone...

~

Heaven forbid . . . Resale!

Oh, I am so tired of hearing people tell me they will never sell . . . then next thing ya know they have found a car they desire more, and low and behold . . . yup, it's gotta go to make room for or provide cash for the next car "I'll never sell." Point is, why shoot yourself in the foot? If every time you do anything to the car, you do it in a fashion that always enhances its value, then are you not doing yourself a favor? The block that came with the car is the original, and yet you rebuild that *other* motor? The car was BRG and it's time to paint and you don't go back original (knock off 30% of the value here for the trouble of throwing a pile of cash at it to make it . . . wrong??? and less valuable!)

~

What's Harming the Hobby?

Hoarders today do more damage to the hobby than all the classics that ever rusted away or are totaled. The act of keeping more cars than you can possibly use damages the hobby in several ways. Firstly, rarity can drive prices up to the point where the once-possible must now be forgotten. Secondly, when the cars are not used and seen, they are again forgotten. Many of the classics one would see at the grocery store 20 years ago have been socked away and the kids have no idea what they are! Thirdly, the lack of use creates a "no need to make spares" problem, and so suppliers not selling widgets certainly aren't going to order more! Personally I think even though I am a most rabid enthusiast, 10 cars is enough; the cars were born to drive and if you find that the battery is always dead and last year you didn't drive it, then let some other "kid at heart" have a chance to play with it! (wouldn't mum be proud of you!) Museums might be ok as long as every car can be made to run with a battery and some gas!

If you are investing and won't be using it regularly, then move "up market" and keep fewer cars. The market has already been ruined for the lovers of the really coolest of the cool especially in Italian cars, and the same thing is happening to the British stuff. No one drives a Ferrari GTO on the street for fun anymore . . . ; don't let that happen to us. I always wanted a DB5 but it's "not gonna happen" now! It would be nice if you can swing it to have a real creampuff of one of the most desirable makes or models like an MG airline coupe or an HRG, perhaps a Riley. When you go that route, you might be in for some pleasant appreciation over the long haul, and it's a safe place to keep some money, but please don't lock it away! Keep it tagged and insured for road use!

SECTION 4:

A LITTLE MORE DETAIL

Joy and Heartache or When the Engine is Seized...

It's not unusual that we find ourselves acquiring a car simply because we "have to" or the deal was too good to pass up. Often, however, there is a very good reason why it was taken off the road those many years ago (it needed, and still does, a very expensive engine rebuild or the body needs a total strip and weld up . . . .) The bad news here is that, yes, it was so expensive in 1976 that Auntie Gin pushed it into the garage, but now it's ten times as expensive to do and is further compounded by the comparatively recent need now to renew virtually everything else (sitting is not good!). In this case, it pays to get the advice of a couple of professionals before formulating an attack plan . . . (I know you promised Auntie a ride as soon as it's running, but there is a logical order to these things!).

Most jobs work like this. First, we assess what is needed on all battle-fronts—body, engine, brakes and interior and, in most cases, you need to start with the body; no point in dropping a fresh engine into a greasy hole like that. Same goes for the interior: paint overspray will make all that leather have to come out again. The paint shop will quickly discover the original color if you don't already know, and this can be the most time-consuming part of the operation. Welding in new panels or fabricating parts can be very time consuming and expensive. You can be doing all your research now while the engine, gearbox and differential can be at your mechanic's being evaluated and/or rebuilt (anything not being rebuilt will, of course, get new seals anyway, right? you *do* want to keep from losing those fluids!). If you are doing a car where you can simply order a replacement interior, then lucky you! For the others, gather photographs of the correct interior (remember those old magazines!) and pass them on to your upholstery guy. I have been using the same upholstery guy, Chip of Chip's Upholstery, since 1988 and he is able—through some sort of magic I fail to understand—to make complete interiors in leather and wool that look exactly like those old photos (except in color, of course!). Finding a guy like him is rare, so ask around a lot before committing. Something like an old Rolls-Royce uses a fortune in leather, and the price of wool carpet is mind numbing (don't be tempted to go vinyl; that's wasting everybody's time and ruining the restoration)!

Matisse, our Bahamian orange cat, on the bonnet of Merrill's beautiful Silver Dawn.

The Cheapest Way to Do Something is to Spend the Most Money

Ok, before you fall out of your chair, let me explain. Does it make sense to fit the recently (and expensively) overhauled engine back into the greasy dungeon of melted broken wires and swelling rotted hoses, just to have the wrecker bring you back as part of your "hose of the month club" or "wire failure of the month club dues" or do you penny up and forgo the likelihood of constant failure? Now as a result of your recalcitrance in the area of hoses, the fresh engine has blown a head gasket . . . brilliant, huh?! Is this a car or not? You can't even let junior drive it for fear it will leave itself somewhere! It's not had the gear box out since Thatcher was in university; the engine is already on the floor, and you don't think it's a good time to drop an extra 100 quid to change the seals on the gearbox? This is what I mean . . . . I have had a V12 E type come in for a clutch and this is no easy feat to change, let me tell you! The client declined to go the extra mile and do the weeping rear main seal on the engine and . . . you guessed it! So . . . ask Mr Wrenchright, "while replacing the Bleany* is there any other small bit near that we should have a peek at?" He might suggest that while renewing all the hoses on your MG B (not just the one that had the look of a small snake that ate a large rat), "we should change the rather aged-looking heater control valve" as it can drip directly onto the distributor cap leaving you roadside and giving you ample opportunity to make new friends! (Did Nigel at Abingdon plan that little "feature"?)

~

Make it Stop before You Make it Go!

Ah, the legendary names. I can close my eyes and see the trackside banners now! Names like "Ferodo" "Mintex." Are they go-fast parts? You betcha they are; they are brake pads and shoes! That's right . . . stopping makes you fast. Out braking another would-be Fangio on the track is not that far from the need to out-brake any "dim bulb" on the street with the resultant increase in safety that may prevent a crease in a fender! Brake boosters and master cylinders, calipers and wheel cylinders are all subject to great stresses and, like the pug in your lap, they need love too. If you are still out there jousting with traffic in your Healey and are relying on the original brake booster, you are not displaying *derring do* but a rather suicidal trait! Same thing with many a cool car. Why, my first E type tried to occupy the same space as a tree; some "economy-minded" individual had attempted to jury rig the brake booster. In this instance, I am glad he did so as it made the car affordable for me to purchase!

~

Fuelishness

This subject is a gas . . . ! Ok, you've read this far, so a joke like that shouldn't surprise you! Old cars tend to come into our possession after long periods of "laying up," and whether this a result of the prior owner's loss of interest or perhaps even his departure to the great garage beyond, laying up is never good for the fuel system. Fuel degrades rapidly (sure the Stabil helps, but it's no replacement for burning the stuff through the engine!). I can't recommend that you let your car sit too long. What is too long depends on how you leave it when you close the garage door. If you drain the carbs and remove all the gas from the tank, set the car on soft top jack stands and remove the battery before pulling the velvet-lined cover over her, then fine . . . almost. But let's assume you are less careful . . . . As the gas evaporates, it leaves a varnish-like "glue" that can hold the floats open. When you attempt to go for your next drive (no doubt you are late already when you douse yourself with gas trying to stop the flow from the stuck float!), this is very dangerous. (Did your electric SU fuel pump stop "tick tick" ticking?) We all know the fire risk. Always have a look under the car or under the "bonnet" (you know that's the proper term, right?) to see if the floats have stuck and are now creating a potential re-enactment of the Hindenburg and upsetting your insurer with some very bad news . . . . Often a stuck float can be rectified by a simple tapping on the side of the float chamber with a properly weighted tool (It's like an honor and a nod to our society that we tend to Frap* or bang things to get them going again; Gramps would be proud!). A small crescent wrench or a medium wrench should suffice to stop the flow (or start the flow in the case of SU fuel pumps). I can't recall how many times I have done this, and, for the foreseeable future thereafter, the car has been fine as long as it's not left to dry out again (some say I might be better if I dried out a bit . . . . I'll drink to that!).

~

Making Sparks and Fire

In an old British sports car nothing is more likely to bring you to a sudden unplanned stop than a failure of the sparks to find their way to the plugs; the overwhelming majority of those failures are the ignition rotor. While there are many proponents of changing your system to an electronic type, the fact is that a points and condenser system, when properly set up and using good quality components as originally supplied, is actually more reliable and considerably less expensive, taking into consideration also that you can change a set of points on the road but you are unlikely to be carrying an extra electronic module. Case in point is my 600,000 mile TR4 (Yes, you read that correctly!). Changing to electronic is damaging to provenance as well: you are, in effect, paying out money to make your vehicle less valuable and less reliable . . . (funny, that's not what the ads for these things say!). The failure is likely going to be the rotor anyway, and you don't change that to something different with a conversion to electronic.

Another frequent failure is spark plugs. Most people don't go to the trouble to fit the correct plugs as recommended by the manufacturer, and most shops fit the plugs they make the best margin on! The simple answer here is in your handbook or original type repair manual. Read it. Find them and accept no substitution; the guy at the car parts store might be a fine fellow, but he should keep his trap shut when you tell him your car came with Champions and you'll wait till he gets them tomorrow. Most often the plugs themselves are not actually the problem (Slapping in a new set can and often does mask an underlying problem that will show itself again soon.) An over-rich mixture is frequently common on things running SU carbs, which is virtually everything that would be the focus of this book. The mixture is generally over-rich mostly due to poorly re-turning chokes and followed closely by owners' constant fiddling (always so self-assured as they cuss their way to a point of "unable to proceed")!

~

The Heat of Internal Combustion

If you are so lucky as to have spark plugs sparking and fuel flowing, then make use of this gift! Keeping the explosions in the cylinders and turning them into forward motion is not really alchemy but close . . . . Too many factors than I am prepared to go into here go into this spell, but all too many guys and gals think they are adept enough to dive deep into the internals for the holy grails of the go-fast set (high compression pistons and special cams), only succeeding in creating a mess and a slower than imagined car in the end. On many occasions I have witnessed a guy with a stock engine of laughably tiny cubic capacity whip the pants off guys with engines that would push a bulldozer. The fact is that a car depends equally on three basic aspects to be "fast": yes, (a) horsepower is nice, but it is relative to the (b) overall weight of the car and (c) its abilities to turn and to stop. So if you are thinking you know so much more than the original design team and "that their Chevy V8" is destined for the now empty hole where your Midget motor threw its rod while you were drag rac'n Ol Luke, then perhaps you should close the book now, grab a wrench and knock yourself out . . . .

High compression pistons, cams, port and polish all sound very nice and, in fact, I do this sort of engine work all the time, but it gets too com-plicated for an owner who has a real job! Let's just make sure the valves are adjusted, the timing is timely and the idle is . . . well, umm . . . not idle!

∽

Music in the Mufflers

Almost the first thing those with a "lead foot" want to do on the car of their dreams is install a "performance" exhaust system (read "louder" here), and, in many cases, the exhaust system needs attention anyway, lest the next speed bump bring the rest of that rusty "noise drain" tumbling out! Most British cars' exhaust systems fit very tightly and some snake through the frame and over the rear axle in something like a love knot and do not not lend themselves well to modification, and, indeed, making the exhaust even slightly louder on a Rolls would be unthinkable! Stainless often seems to be a logical option but don't, unless you really are going to use the car everyday, as the tone of stainless is very different and most of my clients who have made this change, although triumphant in beating any future worries over rust, are shockingly disappointed by the sound. This is not the case with the serious performance systems where quiet is not a consideration . . . .

∽

Tires (tyres)

While many of my clients in the past have arrived at my shop in fine style, in, for instance, Jags costing most of the way to a hundred grand, shod in the correct factory tyres built to maintain triple digit speeds, the majority of owners seem not to see the value of a proper tyre, often riding around on "Maypop" tires. Let's clarify that the price is not the only difference among tyres. The performance capabilities are also a large part of it. Now I have heard it a thousand times so don't bother sounding off with, "I'm not going to go that fast!" That's not the point unless, of course, you are going to go that fast. What I'd be more concerned about is the ability to turn or more likely swerve, as in to avoid something, and this is where tyres' abilities can really separate the straight fenders from the bent, and although most seem to have no problem sporting a new set of premium "shoes" on the Bimmer ("rain car") . . . they will hem and haw endlessly over the cost of new "sneakers" for the car more deserving. Vredestien, along with Avon and others, has been so kind in providing correct sizes that we should not hesitate to spend the extra bucks to make it safe for any errant youngster who might wander into the path and test your reflexes!

~

Keep it between the Ditches!

I've heard many a friend make that pleasant, off-hand comment on parting ways, but really it is rather important, and we should think quite a lot about that! Any loss of steering—a wheel coming off, broken springs or softened shocks (or ones that make crunchy jerky motions), and the ever-frightful steering columns that can twirl within themselves—should be treated like the death threat that it is! I have had guys drive in, that had to stop and put the wire wheel back on twice! Call a wrecker! I don't want to be the one hit by your wheel that is careening down the highway looking for itself! My friend Joe had his actually find a lake! I know of a car that lost two wheels on a single outing (yes, he forgot to tighten the lug nuts!) Some early "impact steering columns" (which, by the way, I think were a brilliant invention, having had a zillion of them pointed at the center of my chest over the years) can have a tendency to wiggle loose. Again people have driven in to show me that if they turn hard the steering wheel, it will turn all the way around with little effect on the direction of the car! (Please call the wrecker!) Wire wheels evoke style and charm, and all those glittering spokes, oh my! But the hub and the way the wheel slips onto it are subject to extreme wear if not routinely greased (much like my wallet) and it may make you feel great with all that spinning bling right there where you can almost, and in some cases actually touch them while you drive, but you will most likely feel quite bad to see the wheel out-accelerate you and hit the jacked up Oldsmobile on much larger wheels belonging to Cranky, the crack dealer (can't drive away now either, can you)!

Shocks are an oft-overlooked and very important thingy! While thundering down the road, you might encounter a rough surface or pothole, and a bad shock could make the resulting motion of the now frantically jumping suspension turn from a joyride to a rollover! Most shocks are available for the same money on "Old Faithful" as on thy modern iron, and when "lever" shocks are needed, there are several excellent rebuilders with ads in *Hemmings*, and elsewhere. Now, "safety fast," like the MG ad used to say, is not just a slogan but your lifestyle. I should point out that the largest safety factor here is you! I have seen all levels of driving prowess from people that can drive Allards (that takes skill!), to well . . . to people that I've asked to call me before they go for a drive so I can fly out of town! You are in control (I hope!) of a serious chunk of metal hurtling down the road at sometimes unsettling speeds and you carry a great shoulder load of responsibility. So, mind the single digit salute you just received from the pedestrian that was blocking the sidewalk and pay attention! (I know the garden gate was right there, but he really shouldn't have to jump for it—lost his cane you know!)

Making it Light, Spin, Flash, or Blow

Most of us have heard some or most of the jokes about Lucas electrics, but I assure you they are absolutely not true; a 50-year-old car can have a broken switch no matter who made it. The problem is more of a "how to" nature, as in how to treat a window switch that has failed to lower a window, for instance (and today I sat in a car made on this side of the pond in which only half of the windows moved and it's only 15 years old!) So, you rock and tap, press and wiggle yet nothing happens. The most common failure in sheer numbers for switch failure is the series three XJ6 (I literally kept about 10 in stock during "those days"). Those switches sat looking up in the centre console and collected every bit of dirt that got near them, and every drop of Coke or coffee went straight into the workings. Simple enough; one could carefully pry the switch out and disassemble it, clean it and put it back together in 10 minutes and all was well again (generally). The same fix continued in the later XJS, but, unfortunately, the 88 and later XJ sedans adopted (modern) "bubble switch" technology, and, as most things "modernized," they no longer lent themselves to repair and the price went up twenty fold! In one case, the switches actually acted as an unstoppable guillotine for one of my customer's arms; the motor was overpowered just short of disaster! So that was only one example, but each car has some more or less common fault and most often they can be made correct and original and work fine (just don't spill Coke in there!).

Often the failure is installed by the unfortunate owner who has fallen ill with a case of "upgrade syndrome." The addition of a battery kill switch can create what appears to be a dead battery. The Hella brand ones don't seem to do this, but fakes and the "green knob" type which clamp directly on the battery are notorious for it! I have had "do it yourselfers" come in at wits' end, who have installed batteries, starters and alternators, trying to cure the problem . . . the whole problem having been the $5 battery switch that they themselves put on! Another example of "upgrade syndrome" that has resulted in countless "tow-ins" over the years is alarm systems. These devices are always ignored when wailing away anyhow! But they are certainly responsible for more "unable to drive" scenarios for owners than for potential thieves. The device either kills the battery or disables the starter, most often an install by an alleged professional. Most of these devices have less quality than a walkie talkie designed for ages 2 to 10! So, while we have this fresh in our minds, and I know some people are concerned about theft, we are now back to some . . . psychology!

The average thief specializing in stealing the whole car knows he is taking a huge risk and needs to profit from his endeavors, so your red XK120 is out of the question. No market to get rid of it and no market for the parts. In short, he wants a Honda! So, what of the idiot thief? Well, he is cutting tops with a pocket knife (if you have been so silly as to use the door lock on a roaster). He will then go through the facia cubby ("glove box") and the arm rest looking for whatever. In the event he means to joyride, your non-locking column cars are so easy to start it's absolutely comical . . . unless you have disabled the engine (no, not that silly battery switch; you did take it off, didn't you?). Simply remove the ignition rotor; have a friend or your mechanic show you how. I even had a friend who used a fake low tension lead from the coil to the distributor! You or your mechanic can install a hidden interrupt switch for the ignition or fuel pump; a simple 3-position switch can be rigged so that when the position for starter is engaged, the horn blows! That'll get him out of your car quick! You may have noted in the movies, the actor reaching under the dash and without looking he hotwires a car . . . not realistic at all. But you may also have seen a movie where the thief shoves a screwdriver with another screwdriver welded to it sticking out sideways as a handle into the ignition switch of a column-lock car and twist it, starting the car as quickly as though he had the key! That is real!

Another example of excellent theft prevention, although not appropriate for most cars, is as follows. I did a self-drive tour of the U.K. and was having dinner north of the Lake District when in came about 15 people in driving gear and quite a few of them were carrying steering wheels. I knew immediately what they were driving--Caterhams and Sevens. I asked and they were delighted to have me go and have a look. It was a club drive, and the U.K. is notorious for joyride thefts, so disabling the car is a must for parking in unsecured places!

～

So Let's Talk about Insurance

My TR4 has been with me since age 14 and that 600,000 miles on her is almost entirely my doing, so it means more to me than the money it might fetch if sold. In 2001- 2002 I took the body off and did a pretty good job of "freshening" it. It looked stunning! Less than two years and fewer than 300 miles later, a nurse looking at roadside scenery hit me from behind at north of 35 mph. I was stopped for a school bus; she never touched the brakes. I was knocked unconscious in the crash, the frame bent, and doors pinned half open. Her insurance adjuster took one look at the car from 20 feet and turned around. "Totaled," he said and was prepared to offer me less money than the paint cost. As a classic car garage guy of many years knows, this is the necessary "step one" to the insurance game. This is what you have to do to get to the people who really take care of claims for classics, unless you have one of the specialist insurers for classic cars or enlist the services of a lawyer . . . . In the end, it took 18 months in my then-favorite body shop and about $16,000 to fix her!

Specialist insurers are an amazing value. You carry the liabilities with your basic auto insurer or homeowner's company, but the specialist covers everything else. I have seen cases where it is significantly cheaper than having all coverage with a standard automotive insurer.

∼

Catching its Stride

It is not unusual for a car to have some sort of failure that then disappears (usually after being towed to my shop where I drive the car into the bay and call the customer, only to discover, ironically, that he says, "it won't start"). In these instances I like to inform my concerned client that it was simply "catching its stride."

Cooling fans can make you hot under the collar. Watching the gauge needle rise is an unhappy pastime. You've already turned the heater on max to pull off some of the engine heat (it is always August when this happens). An expensive new Otter switch and fan motors seem cheap right now, but you had to have that new car cover instead! Don't be tempted to change things; just fix them! The way some people talk, you would think dad and granddad sat in the driveway waiting for the invention of electronic ignition and the alternator! No, they were driving! Yes, before seat heaters; I know, crazy huh? So here we are 142K miles later and the failed part is 35 years old and you wanna complain it was no good! Wake up; have some respect for the poor thing. It gave its little metallic life for you. Clean it up and place it on the shelf in the garage and walk by and thank it once in a while . . . Jeepers!

Headlight switches, turn signals, etc, are all now old enough to smoke and some have exercised that option! Fix them properly rather than modify. It took all those years to fail under the certainly less careful eye of someone else, but you will be more vigilant, won't you?! So no need to "upgrade." I should say more I suppose on the oft-stated misconception that all the electric components on British cars run on "smoke." This is patently false and even though when the "smoke" is coming out of a wire, it is, in fact, the heat of frightened electrons simply rushing to escape some failed component . . . . They are not stupid and this brings me to the brown Spitfire . . . . "The Joe" (as he's known to us) and I were observing a brown Spitfire passing my premises, and he noted that the headlights were quite dim and the tail lights seemed very bright. I then informed him that that car needed a brake job and all the smarter electrons stayed in the infinitely safer rear of the vehicle . . . . While we are on the subject, a battery maintainer will keep legions of brave new electrons ready to sally forth and whisk you on your way, so get one!

∿

Being Seen and Safety

While your chosen mount might be older than seat belt laws and thus relieved of that legal requirement in your neck of the woods, they are still the best insurance we have against injury—other than the good skills to not need them. So invest wisely here. For the more sporting variety there are "aircraft" belts and they do look the business! For most, however, a set of more typical belts will arrest your approach toward the steering column in the event your premonitions let you down about the guy shaving in the Honda in front of you . . . . A solid mounting point is a must: I've seen them pulled out of the bodywork due to undersized backing washers (they should be enormous) and broken because the strap material was sun damaged. Have a pro do it, or at least think long and hard about it, envisioning how the metal or wood will react in the area. On the other hand, sometime before the dimwit applied the shaving cream, you should have made use of the hooters—"Clear Hooters," to be exact (that's a common brand of horn fitted to our cars . . . what did you think?)—and let the nutter know of your imminent impact! Horns are really undervalued by most clients. I do have a few who put honking near the top of the list and wisely so. All joking aside, there are a lot of good horns still around or you can get nice sounding reproductions or even a set of Fiam air horns. That'll make him spray shaving cream all over his interior! You can put two of the Lucas wind tones marker "L" together and have something akin to the sound of a ship's horn in a fog bank when announcing your right to proceed!

You've seen to a proper set of tyres and invested wisely in brakes; making it stop before making it go, is impressively intelligent (you should already be aware of your stopping and turning capability and drive accordingly!).

The lights are a thing of great debate; I favor originality here with a removable supplement for the back window area in cases of cars where a dwarf following in a pedal car four feet astern could not see your tiny tail lights, and, unfortunately, this is all too common with the much older cars. Sometimes the lights are the size of a silver dollar or less with half the incandescent power of a votive candle, and in those cases many owners have succumbed to ads for LED light conversions. As of this writing, they are not much good, and the complexity does not merit the cost or inconvenience of their (imminent) failure, (more due to poor installation than the obvious country of manufacture). The idea never crossed the minds of the original designers to provide for AC, cruise control, heated mirrors, or an ankle scratcher. In most cases, no surprise that things like this usually don't work out and only leave your steed disabled for two weeks before you give up and put it all back to right! When they make a 12V positive ground bulb set in vertical and horizontal forms, perhaps it will be ok for the tail lights but likely not the turn signals. Today, the kits to make LED turn signals work are more trouble than benefit. On the other hand, one thing that is easy and can be done with no modification in most cases is to add a third light which can be ingeniously clipped on to warn following fools of your now-luminous presence, complete with tail and brake lights. Then this third light can be removed for car show presentation!

Headlights should be properly aligned and, in some cases, you can adapt halogen bulbs with no modifications. Many an owner has expressed concern that when stopped at a traffic light at night the lights get dim and then when moving again are bright. Well, just how fast are you going when stopped? No need for the absurd, value-damaging alternator conversion here!

Sadly, windshield wipers rarely work well and in the best of cases seem pitiful, like some chicken has his feet scratching the glass in some kind of fit! And this works in evil concert with the mouse that tries to pant in the direction of the windshield (that would be an accurate description of the defrosters in most cases). So, grab a bottle of Rain X or a similar potion and a good towel in the event you need "defrost," after of course, exhausting all possible efforts to make the systems work and suffering the look on your mechanic's cheerful face when he says you have to stick your fingers in the vent and try to feel the warmth he claims doth emanate from there . . . ("It'll be fine," he says...) and he's right, but you'll be thrilled if you ever are caught in the need for these amazing glass clearing enchantments!

∽

One Last Thing: Buy your Last Car First!

You've now completed your research and successfully rationalized the absolute "NEED" to have that car, and your better half has given up hope (and perhaps seen a lawyer). You've scoured a year's worth of *Hemmings*, and *Collector Car Trader* is your home screen, your "favorites" read like an international expert on classic motor values and availability, the salespeople at Griot's garage know you by name, all your friends come to you for automotive advice, the proper classic insurers have sent their paperwork, you have left bottles of excellent single malt with your mechanic (ahem! . . .), the garage has a new climate control system and the neighbors have retracted the lawsuit about the encroachment of your replica gas station . . . all is well. I do hope to meet you at an event and, thanks to you, another beauty is being saved and properly cared for. Congratulations!

Glossary

Bleany: a fictitious part (often failed)

Nigel and/or Ian: the two fictional characters I credit or blame for most things

Wappy jawed: this is a situation where a car is or appears to be imperfect . . . hence "that mouth on yer E type seems a little funny after ya run over the dog Mearl"

Caddy wampus: see "wappy jawed"

Honeymoon fit: must I explain that? really . . . ?

Wallered out: most often used to describe a bolt hole on the bottom of a generator right before it fell off or a cylinder bore well past need of resleeving

Dog trac'n: a common situation when a car has apparently suffered something like being hit by a train and now seems to go down the road a bit sideways

Frap: an SU fuel pump term—"ya might have ta frap on um a bit ta git'r goin'"

APPENDIX

Like one of those movies where the end comes too soon, you expect the credits to start rolling and people are getting up and making for the exits, but suddenly there's more!

The following portion of the book is just that, made up of previously published articles from various printed and online magazines, so back to your seat and enjoy!

Beware the Idles of March

"What sayeth Robert to thou?" I sayeth, "There is great danger in the forum!" Caesar may have been the first guy you can think of that suffered in the forum, but that was Ancient Rome and we are more concerned with ancient grease!

Car people are tortured every day in online forums, too! Yes, those forums which many of us go to for advice when confounded by some malady that has laid our 4-wheeled chariot asunder . . . . Unfortunately, those would-be soothsayers that we like to think are sages of the socket sets are, in fact, just ordinary guys with so much extra time that they can sit around typing instead of fixing cars. I have seen the worst advice you can imagine in those forums and even some things suggested that are certain to destroy more parts than are already destined for the bin! It is not at all unusual nowadays for a client to start his tale of woe with, "I was looking on the forums . . . . " It used to be that I was the guy who had to find the problem after the client had been to several "cheaper shops" (I never have figured out how it's cheaper to pay several guys a little then pay me too?). Whatever . . . now, people are more likely to have a crack at the problem themselves, if for nothing more than to educate themselves, and I do applaud that! . . . but . . . let me tell you about a recent job on an XK8. This smart young fellow had been to the forums and had, on his own, attempted to find the source of an annoying loud squeak which chirped merrily while driving and stopped completely when the car stopped, running or not. He recounted stories of dash vents and delaminated plastics, hot/cold coefficients and so on but with no luck. I suspected this was one of those jobs that "others" had looked at, so that made it all the more important for me to do a fast diagnosis (nothing like a challenge real or perceived)! So . . . the car not being dropped off yet, I went on the forums for a look and found an unbelievable number of people taking the cars' dashes to bits and having little or no success changing the noises, and numerous reports of mysterious noises, complete with "pay to diagnose and advise" sites giving bizarre advice, not far off from "Caesar, run toward the knife!" (Anyone considering one of those cars should not look at the forums lest their buying feet go from cold to frozen!)

On the appointed day I drove the car and, as described, the noise was loud and made an otherwise pleasant car a candidate for trade in! There was something funny about the noise as it had no apparent point of origin: you couldn't really say, "it's from right about here." It was from everywhere, which of course meant it was from somewhere else! Once I opened the bonnet, my eyes fell directly on the problem, and with a piece of safety wire tied on the shock top bush, the noise was gone! Of course, a new part was ordered for both shocks and the rest is history, but had a more able owner been committed to the advice on the forums, I would have been brought the car on a flatbed tow truck with a disassembled dash . . . a very expensive mistake indeed! So I pray you, leave "Brutus" in the computer or on a bookshelf and "Beware the forums"!

–Robert Morey

Voila--The Cellist is Dead!

I'm sorry if this comes off as somewhat of a rant, but that's because it is . . . .

The act of diagnosing a running problem is not always simple; in fact, like a symphony it is most often NOT simple, and that very statement, "I'm sure it's something simple," made so many times by owners only serves to anger any mechanic. This statement belittles us and, if you must know, makes us more than a little upset! Imagine having someone tell you your job is simple! It's like saying, "I could do this myself but I am taking pity on a wretch like you and will throw you a few shekels from my lofty position, where I cannot be bothered with this trivial thing that is down at your level" . . . . I am careful never to say this to anyone, not the computer guy, the electrician, the doctor, etc. The very fact that I must enlist assistance means it is not simple.

One of my favorite things to do, build engines
(here a truly fantastic restoration for Tracey Hutchins).

Let's have a look at the "simplicity" of diagnosis . . . . By example let's think of our lovely car as a symphony and it's just not right; out of tune, lacking harmony . . . something is amiss and we can't get it in tune. Sure there is the possibility that only one thing is missing, (would Simon Rattle put up with such?!), and we discover without much ado that, in fact, the cellist is dead!, and having carried her out by a backstage door to the sad murmuring of the crowd, we replace her and the music is perfect (except the flute player—he's always been a bit off, hasn't he?!) . . . . Fine, in this case all is well again. Now let's assume that the symphony is not a standard 40 to 115 players but instead thousands and that they are all aged and many have never had any care at all, cannot play well, and are hiding behind others and behind walls in places difficult to get to and have had years of other so-called "conductors," competent and very much otherwise, trying to root them out and replace them with good players or, worse, just patch them up to play a bit longer . . . . Now we have a clearer picture, don't we? So the string section has a few broken strings but still sounds rather nice; the drums however only strike when the mood strikes them. I hope for a few more dead cellists for your sake but give us the benefit of the doubt here: it could be much much more complex and in some cases not worth the effort! . . . . "Not worth the effort!!" Really? Yes and here's why . . . . Let's say you are called in to repair a long chain and there is one broken link on an otherwise perfect shiny chain. You are, upon completion, the hero and all the crowd applauds you, but suppose the chain has been heavily worn and many links are suspect, so you change the worst one and shortly thereafter another link breaks, then another . . . You are then a scoundrel and the rumor mill will resonate with your failure!!! . . . yes, "Not worth the effort"! as what will suffer here most is not the client with the rusty chain but the harmony of your reputation . . . .

Rant over . . . it's ok now.

–Robert Morey

Parts Pirates

"Yo ho ho and a bottle of 'automotive snake oil'"???

It seems in today's "buy it now" world of eBay and Paypal, we can now have useless junk sent directly to our front door without so much as picking it up and saying, "$50 for that?!" Yes, ladies and gentlemen, in most cases today's manufacturers of automotive junk should simply set up a dumpster at the end of the assembly line and save us the trouble of throwing away that widget that isn't even close to "fit for service." Just type in what you are looking for to get your "2002 Smokesabit coupe" back on the road, and you'll be treated to scores of "parts pirates" ads bent on getting you to use their search engine because "you can find it here"—only to go in circles typing all your info simply to discover, "No you can't find it here!" (Tip: if it doesn't come up as a direct link when you google a part, it will not come up through a parts search engine).

So, before you allow Blackbeard to swing a sword through your bank account, listen up! Know what you are looking for. If you type in "water pump," you will get millions of results! So, (fingers off the keyboard!—it's just an example) be very very specific! For instance, "1999 Jaguar XJ8 water pump aluminum impeller for sale." Then be sure to read the WHOLE ad. That part might be made in and coming from the other side of the world; you want the one made in a country known for quality and preferably to have it on your door in a couple days—not a couple weeks. Now read at least five more ads for the same part and compare manufacturers and prices. I'm tell'n ya, it's crazy out there! And check locally, too, and here's why! I had a job recently that needed a fairly common part. There are three parts stores near me, two that advertise as being "bargain type stores" and one regular parts store . . . . The first one I tried (regular type store) had the part for $65 and could have it to me in an hour; the first "bargain store" could get it to me in two days for almost $300! And the last store could not get it at all. Online, an average was $45 for admitted "very distant" origin reproduction (and I should mention the dealer had them for $150, yes half that of the bargain store!) The car's owner opted for the cheap-and-here version as most would . . . point being that the internet is not always the way to go! So "Avast Mateys!"—not shopping around can have the parts pirates pillaging your pocket!

–Robert Morey

The Disenchanted Wizard

The Wizard sat still, trying to shake off the sluggish mind of sleep, trying to move slowly every little muscle starting at the toes and working up. This seemed the safest way to get all the old parts moving and prepare himself for a day of the new spells, "Ha the new spells!" What a far cry from the magic of his childhood, so sad an excuse for magic; again he could not move. Sitting another 10 minutes and moving all the parts of his fingers, he finally got up for a small breakfast to stop the hunger. This simple act brought up the courage to get on with it; the coffee brought about some more thinking, but it was mostly sad.

He looked about the room and there were not more than a few inches anywhere on the walls where there did not hang a tool or a part and all the available shelves were filled to overflowing with the potions of his craft. There were of course the favorites: the degree wheel, the porting and polishing tools, the CC'ing rig with its clear glass so covered with dust it was no longer transparent, the scales so long unused they had taken on the appearance of a prop in a movie. This was a shop of the old magic and every corner proved it. The decorations were all of old magic from the time of glory, the time of pride and the time when all that magic had a feeling of permanence. Now there is none of that and the children know not of what he speaks; talking to the young he can tell he speaks to them in an old tongue full of words they do not comprehend: "end for end and total weight," "setting the cam timing with offset keys." The tools around the shop were bizarre to them too—"Fettle" . . . it trims sharp edges from combustion chambers?!, Why?? . . . no need to go to the trouble to do this lesson again for some child who will never need it . . . .

The Wizard slumped over his desk and wondered if the coffee was still warm, the only pleasure he would likely have today. Then on the phone a familiar voice and a request for old magic—an MGA needs a fresh engine—oh how fun!, a real job and being allowed to do some of the old spells. The Wizard fantasized for a while about a patron who would have him build a Lotus Twincam like the old days when they would be waiting in line for a build complete with all the magic spells and some of his own making. The Wizard caught himself and proceeded with the paperwork and parts chasing, seeing that the cost of old Magic is a bargain compared to the new, plastic parts more costly than steel ! Amazing how the world has changed. He cursed the tiny computers that so many had polluted the old cars with—an ignition module in a 50s car. What a foolish move! Not even a puff of smoke when it fails and they all believe when it does that it must be the only one that ever failed and are told those lies by the suppliers. The Wizard would always nod at the glass jar on the shelf he kept full of the dead modules to try to make them understand: "the new magic is not good magic for the old cars." If he saw any glow of understanding in the customer, then he would point out the other atrocities that had been wrought on their car: alternators and the ground conversion it required, modern headlights to see pointlessly farther than necessary, LED lights which look so wrong and require so much change to the car that any failure in the system now requires a fantastic amount of work to correct (compared to the simple act of replacing a bulb), the gear reduction starters (a curse indeed!). What a foolish thing to put a pathetic low quality thing like that on a wonderful car; a pile of those also live here under a bench.

The Wizard feeling better now remembered some of the good jobs, where a wise owner removed all traces of modern equipment and made his car correct; the only failing in a totally correct car is that it is much less likely to come visit his shop! But still this is not a problem. What is a problem is when so many insist, "I need AC," "put the top down," "I need iPod interface . . . !" "Are you mad? You can hear nothing in a roadster from the stereo!" "Get earphones and don't modify the car!" and with this admonishment that fell on no one's ears, he realized he had again been talking out loud to himself . . . . He settled in again to reminisce. In his mind he could see his mentor the great Wizard so many years ago— when all the great marques were still sold new—and feel the importance of his teaching; he remembered that the other apprentice went on to work with the Bentley Le Mans team. How he would have loved that!; he thought of another wizard where he studied and the great stories of F adventures that wizard told, the engine building magic he learned from him, magic used by the greats—Colin Chapman, Enzo Ferrari, McLaren, and so on. He looked up again and saw across the shop a '67 Lotus, '53 Aston Martin, and the start of it all—his '62 TR4. A smile formed and all was well again!

—Robert Morey

The Zombie Apocalypse!

Your "modern iron," "rain car," "grocery getter"—whatever you want to call it—is turning you into a Zombie! Yes, it's true. A lazy one at that! Auto wipers, auto lights, seats that move at the touch of a button, navigation that responds to voice command! They even put controls right on the steering wheel so movement of your muscles is almost gone. Even the kids are not safe: the TV screens in your headrests are part of the evil plot. The kids won't know what's going on outside the car unless you feed the backup camera into the TV headrests! The list goes on . . . !

The start was the automatic transmission and few took offense, but they got the Zombie plan up to speed (although electronically limited to prevent engine damage): "satellite navigation" now with crash information upload and "EMS alert system," memory seats, memory mirrors, "parking proximity alert," "dual climate control" (there're TWO climates in my car?!), "DSC" (dynamic stability control), "ABS" (anti-lock brake system), proximity keys, remote locks, remote start, automatic high beam control! Heck, you can get the CDC and MSN with your mobile cloud/WiFi uplink "bluetooth" (all those wasted dentist trips!) And here comes "auto park" and "auto drive"!

You already barely need to move to operate a modern vehicle. Soon, we'll read articles about people still driving that have been dead for days! I don't know about you, but I'm getting in my stick shift car with windup windows and manual seats and escaping! But I'm taking my smartphone in case I need to ask Siri how to escape Zombies . . . .

–Robert Morey